Branches

Mossy Creek Press

Branches
ISBN: Softcover 978-0692649688
Copyright © 2016 by Suellen Alfred

All rights reserved. No part of this book may be reproduced or transmitted in any form or by any means, electronic or mechanical, including photocopying, recording, or by any information storage and retrieval system, without permission in writing from the publisher.

To order additional copies of this book, contact:

Mossy Creek Press
1-423-475-7308
www.mossycreekpress.com

Mossy Creek Press is an imprint of Parson's Porch & Company (PP&C) in Cleveland, Tennessee. PP&C is an innovative organization which raises money by publishing books of noted authors, representing all genres. All donations from contributors and profits from publishing are shared with the students of Carson – Newman University.

Branches

In Fond Memory of

Richard Campbell Pettigrew, who taught me poetry
at Carson-Newman University

Arthur E. Waterman, who taught me poetry
at Georgia State University

Table of Contents

Introduction

Branches	11
Request from a Poet at an Oral Reading	12

Love Lost and Found

Ruth	15
Again	16
Quarrel	17
Still	18
Self Deception	19
Enough	20
A Sunday Afternoon	21
A Smile	22
After	23
The Geology Lesson	24
Halloween Poem	25
Laundry	26

Nature

Country Morning	29
Mountain Spirit	30
Call and Response	31
Cummings Falls	32
The Shadow	33
October Heat	34
Transition	35
Flourish	36
Surcease	37
It Rained	38
This Small Moon	39
When the Moon Has Left to Shine on Other Shores	40
The Snow	41
False Prophets	42
Winter Solstice	43
The Coming Light	44

Creatures

Winter Birds	47
Owl: 4:00 A. M.	48
Woodpecker: 12:00 Noon	49
A Poem for Bones the Dream Dog	50
Affirmation at Panther Creek	51

Family

News at Sundown	55
The Better Part of Wisdom	56
The Better Reader	58
After Supper	60
Connection	62
Balancing the Books	64
Legs Together	65
Advice to a Slow Learner	66
Rectification	67
Antiphony of Judgment for Two Voices	69
A Patch of Sun	70
The Stranger	71
Move on to the River	72

Spirit

Order for the Visitation to the Sick	75
Song of the Agnostic	76
Letter to St. Paul	77
The Breath of God	78
Two Witches	79
October One	80
From All Saints to Advent	81
My Layers Fall Away	82
Suellen Alfred Information	83

Introduction

Branches

Like our own capillaries,
tiny branches reach into the vacant space around them.
Light – air – water – even snow
sustain them.
Their movements unobserved,
they inch, surreptitious, into the air,
curve toward the window,
stare in at us
as if to say,
"How sadly self-contained you are."

Request from a Poet at an Oral Reading

When I read to you,
I want the sound of this poem to match the sounds
in your own head,
sounds that came down to you through your mother
before you were born,
sounds that were bred
by ancient elders in the fog of eons gone from the dark of earth's
womb,
the caves,
the dwelling places of our kin
whose corporeal form in us has blossomed,
      fully human.

So tell me that you hear those sounds,
a language that connects us both to common visions
and to comely dreams.

Love Lost and Found

Ruth

"I cannot see how we should," she said.
He stared, silent, his eyes,
a blue that cracked and sparkled,
like ice on a pond, locked in winter.
"What is the purpose? How will it bless us both?"
Her question hung in the silence of his refusal.
He had only half an answer,
the half that knew the profit was all his.

His irritation crossed his face,
a ripple on a wind-swept pond
in springtime after the ice was gone. She waited. He wondered.
He hesitated.
She left the room without a word
– not his, not hers –
a woman wrapped in her own resolve.

He knew the world had shifted,
had turned from black and white to complex gray. The ancient loyalty
of Ruth no longer held.
He faintly heard the alteration of the ancient scripture "Wither thou
goest, I will not . . . unless . . ."

Again

You stood framed in the doorway, leaning like a person quite at
home amid the Spartan spaces
of a sometime scholar.
You graced the doorway
with your brown and gleaming presence,
angular,
as one who knows how much it means
 to stay and take her chances with
all she does not know
and cannot understand.

Quarrel

The rain roared
and so did we;
roared in unison,
we three:
you and me
and the rain.

Still

Time has crept past us like the velvet secret moving of the night.
And you have moved to other days.
The memories bring a smile,
the stones you walked,
the steps you climbed,
the doors you gingerly unlocked are here.
And you are gone.

Still.

Self-Deception

I am going through my life pretending
> you were never in this kitchen.
>> It was made for one.
>> But we two moved within its confines
>> like dancers who knew their parts and never missed a beat.
>> Your body was light.
>> It moved to my impulse like the flight of a bird
>> that moves to an unseen cosmic rule
>> as old as Eros.
>> I spun you around until
>> you asked that the spinning in your head and in your heart
>> be still.

I am going through my life pretending
> we never lit the candles
>> on the landlord's table (left here because
>> he had quite other lives to live).
>> We shared our simple meals with simple wine
>> and smiled almost in tune.

I am going through my life pretending
> the sound of Chopin did not make our bodies
>> surge and move in rhythms almost contained.
>> We struggled with impulses
>> we knew we could not own.

I am going through my life pretending
> you did not sit
>> in this spare room,
>> the room you called your own.
>> You leaned your raven head against the chair
>> and said, "It is so peaceful here."
>> You read the poems of Alice Walker:
>> "Expect nothing. Live frugally by surprise."

I am going through my life pretending
> you will be there when I call.

Enough

I am trying to make the birds enough
to fill the space.

The rain crow who rides the wire
and coos her mournful message
to a gray and dimming sky.

The wren who is not here this fall
but will be in her house
when summer comes.

The cardinal who brightens up the evergreen
and may see fit to build his nest among the cones
next spring.

The blue bird, whose image flies now
only in my memory of bluer skies,
will be here too.
I must prepare her house.
. . .the birds enough . . .

A Sunday Afternoon

What was the glee that sat just behind your face?
We came to the very edge of what we both wanted –
desiring and fearing –
loving each other with our eyes, wanting to do the best thing,
 needing to do the passionate thing.

The promise of consummation surged beneath
our patter, filled our laughter, tinged the air
and our throbbing bodies.
We could not stop smiling.

The conversation shifted easily;
I was as surprised as you were
when I said my desire echoed yours.

We swung into a healthy gait up the forest path,
arms around each other,
laughing at our foolishness.

We warmed ourselves in one another's smile,
knowing that we could – if we would –
make each other's bodies sing.

The creek was ours.
It cooled only our skin.
Your hair matched its gleam.
Its brightness danced in your eyes.

A quick goodbye kiss was all we would allow.
It still melts in my mouth.

I cannot stop smiling.

A Smile

The sun through the trees
and the scent of new grown grass
    in the twinkling afternoon.
The memory of last night's rain,
staccato sounds on tin,
    and the touch of your dry warm hand.

After

Sheets lay in a wrinkled heap.
    Moaning like a worker with a heavy load,
        the fan limped around its dusty hub, barely cooling our
bodies
        gleaming with the glaze of satisfaction.

The open window offered up more hope
        ushering in the ocean breeze.

The salt air and the ancient ocean roar
        echoed the tastes and sounds
        of what had come an hour
        before the earth moved.

The Geology Lesson

My Mohs' Scale of the heart
    slid
        from
            ten
                to
                    one
                        when
                            you
                                took
                                  my
                                      hand.

Halloween Poem

When the afternoon moved from the top of the day,
we moved with it into another way of knowing.
All Hallows Eve
found us without masks
        and without apprehension.

We tricked the moon
who worked her ancient magic
on our hearts and in the fiber
of our thirsty bones.
The ghosts, the shadows we
no longer could deny,
rose like great specters in the middle of our souls.

We howled as wolves throw back
their trusting heads
and offer up their arching throats with songs to silent spaces
in the cold and snowy beauty stunned with mist.

We treated one another to the rhythm of the tides.
The ancient shapes of mountains all around us
echoed the shapes our bodies offered up in greeting
awash in gentle undergoing
        undulations.

Sweet love made all the sweeter
by the soft unbridled movement of the selves we did not know
and did not dare deny.

Laundry

I am folding this shirt straight from the dryer,
warm and fragrant.
Soon it will take on your special scent,
the scent of earth and new mown grass
that clings to you
even after the shower.

You will button it over your strong shoulders.
We will get dressed and go to dine with friends
and smile across the table,
you, in your fragrant shirt fresh from the dryer,
smiling as though it were a royal robe.

Nature

Country Morning

Sprung up inside the silence of the night,
    while the known world slept,
        moist white webs grace the grass.

One web hovers in the breeze,
    the spider at the center,
        a glistening symmetry in the morning light.

Crows rattle in the distance.
    Their far-flung dialogue comes through the air
    from shimmering trees.

The sun moves slowly through the purple plumb
    that chatters with its unseen guests,
        as shadows shorten toward a shining day.

Mountain Spirit

The Mountain Spirit of the Smokies came to sit beside my ghosts
and color now their faces with her own silent charm,
an elfin joke from Pan, a layering up of images
more powerful than the ones I came to lose.

And now I see their faces in the
hemlock and the pine
and hear their voices in the twinkling stream,
a composition made of wood and leaf and blood and bone.

The Mountain Spirit weaves the yarn of what I bring
into her tapestry of green and gold,
and I am left to carry home the woof of wood and stream,
the warp of what I've shuttled through this woven life.
More fully haunted still.

Call and Response

You can shout it to the river,
but the hills will shout it back.
They have heard it all before.

Cummings Falls

The blue insisted its way from the sky into the day that fell around us
as Cummings Falls fell
                      from
                              one
                                    level
                                          to
                                              the
                                                    other,
moving liquid lace
                      flowing from terrace
                                        to terrace,
                                                            stratified beauty
in a roar that tumbled to the sky.

The Shadow

The sun casts shadows of a moving path across this page.

Two points meet on this line:
    the pen filled with ink records this thought;
    the shadow filled only with itself
        moves as the pen moves,
        lives only in the light,
        dies in its own darkness,
        takes life from things that fall between it

    and the sun.

It mocks the forms of concrete things.

October Heat

Ripe with the menses of a storm, the air refuses
        to release its burden to the ground.
The humidity thickens in the graying light.
My forehead moistens
        in the twilight of a hot October evening.
The month has traveled back in time to August,
        the month of constant heat and endless hopes of rain.

A reversal of ordinary expectations,
        unsettling in its failure to move the season forward
        toward frost and reddening leaves.

This month behaves as if it fears the future,
        the color brown that sends the green away,
        the dark, the cold,
        the raucous wind that robs us
        of the warmth our bodies work so hard to generate
        and to maintain.

This cannot last. The tilting earth will have its way.

November will do October's job, and more.
We will respond and marshal all the heat we have
        and all we can create from browning trees
        that shed their leaves and life - their sacrifice for us.
        We will work alchemy to change the elements.
        We will transform the wood to light, to fire
        against the dark, the cold,
        against the blistering wind.

Transition
San Antonio, June 1999

Where shall we go amidst this heat
that bears down on us unrelenting?
It wraps its warm wet sufferance around us like a pall.
It shimmers in the air and rises from the land in quivering mirages.
But, oh, in the distance
I hear the thunder,
the fanfare for a new arrival. The rain is on its way.

Flourish

Silent now,
the air holds its breath.
The sky turns green to black,
a soporific calm,
a deception
that draws us
toward unwarranted expectation.

Faint,
a whisper,
then a whine,
threading out of the west,
the distant wind announces
 the storm is on its way.

Surcease

It's the first hint we've had of another season
        since way before July.
The heat has made its home
        in our bodies and our minds.
The dog pants and stays close to the water bowl.
Strange insects chatter the mercury up the scale,
        and the spread is thrown on the floor
        this morning.
But today it rained
        a slow rain,
          filling the bird bath with more than enough,
          filling the pond up to the brim,
          filling the sky with thunder and with surcease.

It Rained

It rained
against all possibilities.
The oak tree behind the Hall
vocalized the coming of the breeze staccato pointed sound
beneath the gray
the wind rose
the cold came
the damp
slid its way
into our jackets
gave up the
hope of staying dry.
It rained.

This Small Moon

What is this small moon
that hovers over the gloomy scene
about the horizon?
Does it illuminate the lavender hills
or do they shine from their own sweet mystery?

When the Moon Has Left to Shine on Other Shores

When the moon has left to shine on other shores and we are left
to stumble in the dark to find our way as best we can
with artificial light too yellow and impure when cast against
our memory of the silver absent moon,
this time of darkness scurries us indoors.

Drawn by the fire and candlelight, we huddle in our homes
against the cold, against the frightening dark
with steaming cups of conversation in search of human warmth,
charmed by the heat and human voices that curl around our isolation
and keep us safe.

The Snow

The snow
is white
delicate
in its singular beauty deceptive.

False Prophets
November 2

The cold fog is here.
All saints have gone to their graves
and left the leaves to fall alone without the visitation of the dead.

The wind blows rain against the house.
The day turns gray with age.

It is a dark time.

Plump robins shiver in the naked tree.
Their pale orange breasts puff out
like grafted peaches on a barren limb.
Mute strangers in the hovering mist,
they carry on their hearts the color of the sun,
reflected only there and nowhere else.

They are false prophets
who foretell a Spring that will not be here soon.

Winter Solstice

The snow falls flake on flake on flake,
a spectral plumb line straight down to the ground.
No wind disturbs her unrelenting journey
to the earth
to which we all return
when it is time.

"The darkest evening of the year,"[1]
the moon in slumber does not lift her head,[2]
withholding all she has to show of silver landscapes that remain
obscured.

And we are left without the light
in darkest peace
in shades of hope
in sheaves of faith
in clear imagination of what will be revealed.

A strengthening sun will show us
what we know has been here all along.
 The world is turning toward the light.

---

[1] A line taken from Frost's "Stopping by Woods on a Snowy Evening."
[2] A modification of the last lines in Shakespeare's *Romeo and Juliet:* "The sun for sorrow will not lift its head."

The Coming Light

We have hidden from you
O Light, and you from us.
On the darkening side of the world
we burrowed into warm dark homes
against the coldness that comes with your leaving.
But now we see you coming 'round again,
inch by inch – a minute at a day;
and slowly the bulbs and roots
with whom we slept are stirring.

We have done well in our dens and burrows in our dormant fertile time.
We have done well to sit,
to wait in silent darkness,
to fill our souls with night
and give our spirits time to rest.

Our waiting has prepared us for this time.
We are the heliotropes.
We turn our faces to your stirring warmth,
and each new minute of a lighter day
will make us able to become new.

Creatures

Winter Birds

Beside the cardinals and the jays,
the doves are here in muted beauty.
They bob their heads in round-eyed affirmation.
Their staccato beaks clean up the seeds
dropped from the feeder to the ground
by that one careless crow.

They feast on sunflower seeds whose towering offspring
will arrive in seven months with August heat.
But now the snow survives the mercury's puny height;
and, grateful for free abundant meals,
the doves dine well in aviary unawareness of the peace they bring.

Owl: 4:00 a. m.

I hear you whooing out there in the mist,
old owl,
ancient Wise Bird hidden in the blushing dogwood.

The cool of the predawn hour wraps around your song.
Even through the closed window,
      sealed in a study full of silent books,
        I hear your gentle alto resonating voice.

And I sit at my desk,
the presumption of judgment bleeding through
my red pen,
      giving partial credit or full or none at all
        to tiresome student answers on a folded page.

I sit among the leaves that your trees died for.
You sit in the magic untold wonder of October,
      among the leaves that only now are turning red,
      dying a natural death for the Fall of the season,
      not for the Fall of man.

Keats had his nightingale.
I have my owl.
And I am more than half in love with easeful life – not death –
and have no wish to "fly away with thee."

I ask that your pure vowel sound of ooo,
      like the meditation mantra of an insulated monk,
      be not the call of death but more a call to life and growth,
      even as the unruly hair that shags my head
      turns grayer as the leaves turn brown.

Woodpecker: 12:00 Noon

And now it is you,
        midday,
the drummer in the wood,
the percussionist,
pecking your way toward culinary delight out there where last night I
heard the owl.

You bring my head up quick.
Your tattoo makes me
move out to the shining day
for no real cause except to say
I'm here.

A Poem for Bones, the Dream Dog

Low-slung, unable to rise barely above the tall grass
that fills your belly full of fleas,

you lie close to the earth
and dream -
a mock chase of shaking limbs and subdued whimpers.

Does the dog muse visit
you in your earth-bound dreams
like rainbows
falling, unexpected, on the ground,
distilled by beveled glass
that brings them down to earth
to bless us in surprise?
Are you visited with poems as I?

Cramped by lack of language,
 bereft of any translator,
your poem is locked inside
an aging brindled body.

And only I
have a small glimmer
of the treasure in your heart.

Affirmation at Panther Creek[3]

We had climbed the ridge,
my old dog, Bones, and I,
to stretch our muscles
and exercise our lungs
before the dark would put us both to bed.

Through the gloom and waning light I saw them, three deer stone still,
in frozen vigilance,
as if a stonemason had planted them
in case a casual hiker and her dog
were disappointed
in searching for the real thing.

Deer and forest wore the same brown coat,
each a reflection of the spirit in the wood.
I wasn't sure.
Were they a mirage?
A conjuring of my own vain hope?

Bones knew.
He usually was a rooting restless hound,
not likely to stand still
for much of anything.
But not today.

His nose found them first,
and then his eyes.
The deer returned his gaze
in cautious curiosity.

He stiffened like a pointer,
responding with some ancient
inbred instinct long since layered in his brain,
 though not in his stocky confirmation.
He didn't move.

We stood in rapt attention,
charmed by beauty and deer magic,
and matched their strong silence.
And then I knew my eyes had told the truth.
And then they vanished with the dying light.

[3] A version of this poem appeared in Margaret Britton Vaughn and Suellen Alfred. *Southern Voices in Every Direction.* Bell Buckle, TN: Bell Buckle/Iris Press, 1996, p. 42.

Family

News at Sundown

He come up over the hill and started down the east side toward me.
Couldn't see him good because the sun was at his back,
a purty sight,
the sky full of colors,
the sun easin' its way down behind the hill
and him dark as the shadow that led him down the path,
walking in that easy long legged way of his.
I could tell by the way he was a-walkin' that he was a-smilin', headed
home with good news.

The Better Part of Wisdom

Well, I never saw anything to beat it.
He come over that hill holdin' on to the plow
with an iron grip
and that mule a-pullin' and a-jumpin'
around, and a-kickin' and a-fartin' like a lunatic.
I never saw Clyde Claiborn run that fast
or holler that loud.
      – you could have heard him clear to Clinton.

"Whoa, girl," he said a hundred times.
That mule run through the fence,
      knocked down the posts,
      run across the road,
      through another pasture field,
      Clyde right behind her a-yellin' and a-sweatin'.

That mule run clean into the river.
Then she stopped just like she'd run out of steam,
      wall-eyed and breathin' heavy.
Clyde, he just follered her into the water.
It come plumb up to his knees.
But he held on to the reins
      and waded up to that mule real slow and calm.

"Good girl," he said, all quiet and gentle.
Petted her like she was a kitten
      and hollered for me to bring him some chewin'
      tobacco.
I took it down to the river.
He chewed it a little while and made it into a poultice.
Put it on the biggest knot I'd ever seen on a mule's head.
It was a bee sting got her upset and all.

But pretty soon she quieted down
and the two of them come up out of the river
back to the barn, plow and all. "All in a day's work," he said.
"But Molly needs to settle down. We'll plow tomorrow."

I never seen a man with so much sense.

The Better Reader

If'n you can read this
paper,
>you're a sight better off than me and them boys
>down the road
> who couldn't read the signs of the
>times if Jesus came back,
>they're so ignorant
>and all.

But I can read some things
that you can't,
>like the wooly worms
>and the fogs in August and the hornets
>close to the ground,
>telling me about
>the winter that's
>on its way
>even in this heat
>and dust.

And I can read
the signs for
>planting
>when the moon is up
>or down depending on the time of month.
>Or full or not
>at all.

And I can read
>the look on
>my daughter's face
>whose got my eyes
>and his chin.
I can read her face
>when I tell her

      she's the smartest
      and the sweetest
      one of all.

Reading the signs
    and the
      faces
    is all I need.

After Supper[4]

We walked out on the porch to ease our way from the heat of the kitchen.
You want a piece of pie?
No, mama, I can't eat another bite.
You don't want a piece of pie? It's chocolate.
Well maybe just a little piece.
An ancient dialogue.
Food for fondness and affirmation,
care and gratitude and guilt
in a wedge of chocolate and meringue.

The shadows inched their way into the dark evening,
 and the crickets sang their atmospheric song.
They say you can tell the temperature
by how many times a cricket chirps.
So they say.
And by what the needle on the thermometer says.
We smiled. Sound and sight. Old and new.
The air chilled only enough for long sleeves,
not a heavy jacket, not the one that hung
on the peg by the door,
the one that sheltered George from the morning mist at milking.
The coffee tasted good in those old heavy cups cracked with wear.
No need to throw those cups away, she said.
They do just fine.
Better save your money, honey.
You never can tell what might happen.

The breeze rose of a sudden,
full of the scent of fertilized fields,
and caught the maple by surprise.
It shuddered at the thought
that the wind would assault it so
without announcement.

It'll rain tomorrow for sure.
See that ring around the moon?
We need it. The grass is gettin' brown.
 I love the rain.
It makes me feel at peace
under a safe roof in a warm house,
 thankful.
By the fire I can rock and read.
And remember.

[4] A version of this poem appeared in Margaret Britton Vaughn and Suellen Alfred. *Southern Voices in Every Direction*. Bell Buckle, TN: Bell Buckle/Iris Press, 1996, p. 41.

Connection

For Joe
"Come on," you said.
"Let's catch the sunset."
Like our parents before us
we were once again on the lake,
your boat moored at a point that faced the sun.

While the sun was high
we scoured the point for wood, calling each to the other.
"Find any?"
"Need some help?"
"This one's too big."
"Come on and bring the saw."
Call and response,
a duet of happy toil.

Those words, "come on"
captured fragments of our childhood, memories of your boyish invitations,
"Come on" – let's shoot tin cans.
"Come on" – let's wire up these phones.
"Come on" – let's go water skiing.
"Come on" – let's ride the go-cart.

You were the captain of adventure;
I the eager girl who went along.
Soul mates all our lives,
children of sister-soul mates all their lives.
Now – we are two sixty-year old cousins like brother and sister
two sides of the same soul.

Your quick mechanical dysgraphic mind,
my wordful innumeracy,
both with the same immeasurable unutterable

aptitude for beauty
drawn to a kaleidoscopic setting sun.

We laid a fire for a later time
when we would want its light and warmth,
against the gloom and damp that would soon surround us
 in the absence of the disappearing sun.

Then through the woods we went
to the western facing shore,
camera and camping chairs in hand,
like tourists rushing to a rare and special site.
And sat.
And watched.
And talked about the mystery of a simple setting sun
attended by the ghosts of sister mothers long since gone
and with us still.

Balancing the Books

0
Zeeeero is an **even** number,
Even when preceded by a single digit
        in base ten,
Even when it follows itself in a long line
        of abundance.
Even when it stands

        alone,

Even when you've got it all,
Even when you ain't got nothin',
Zeeero is an **even** number.
0

Legs Together

Keeping your legs together,
Young Lady,
    is good advice
      in lots of places.

In skiing,
    skis parallel
    knees bent
    head down
    otherwise you'll straddle a mountain of pain.

In canoeing,
    both feet in the boat not
    both feet out,
    otherwise you'll drift;
    your reach will exceed your grasp and you'll fall.

In love,
see above.

Advice to A Slow Learner Who Hasn't Figured It Out

How long will it take you to figure out
that when you lie down with a son of a bitch,
you come up with a hell of a lot more than fleas?
You come up with a serious case of second thoughts
and maybe a breathing lasting reminder
that brings with it
a lifetime of life or death decisions
and regrets either way you go.
Better stay on your feet and wonder about it.

Rectification

No, no, Missie.
You ain't goin' back to that son of a bitch, him and his drinking -
Hell, he ain't worth the time it would take
to cut him up for stew
tough old root hog that he is.
No, honey, you stay right here with me
and let him holler himself clear to Knoxville.

No ma'm, it ain't your fault.
No man worth his salt would ever
hit a woman, especially a girl as good as you,
no matter what she says to him.

Hell no. He better not come sniffin' around this house, by god.
His butt won't be the first one
that's high tailed it off this land
with buckshot burnin' his behind.
And if you think I'm afraid to use this shotgun,
just go down the road a piece
and talk to Lomey Ann Carter's boy.
One night last year he come prowlin' around over here
trying' to steal him a watermelon.
The only thing he toted home was a tail full of lead for his trouble.
And that boy never hit a lick at a soul in his life.

But that sorry thing you married
ain't good enough to wipe Luke Carter's butt.
He's a charmer all right, pretty as a polecat and just as foul.
 I know he fooled you good.
Almost fooled me too with his purty smile
comin' around here grinnin' like a mule eatin' briars
and his "Yes m'amin'" me all over the place
and his tellin' you and me both what a fine girl you are
and how he'd give you the moon if he could get it.

Moon, my foot! You'd been a hell of a lot better off
if he'd brought home a paycheck once in a while
 instead of pouring his money down his throat
 through a bottle of John Barleycorn.
When he is full of likker
there ain't no skunk in Campbell County
can match the stink that comes pourin'
out of that son of a bitch.
O, I know how fine he is when he is sober.
But, hell, girlie, you can't depend on him to stay that way.
You made a mistake, girl.
Everbody does once in a while,
but comin' over here to your Aunt Mossie's house
was the first step in rectifying the damage.
If you go back over there to that bastard again
you'll start down that long dark road of one mistake after another
until you end up in the hospital
or he ends up in the grave
ater I've splattered his brains all over
Hell and half of Hogan's creek.

Don't you go flouncin' back to that snake in the grass.
You just set yourself right down here at the kitchen table
and get you a piece of apple pie and a glass of sweet milk.
Then you put that little butt of yours in the bed
where you can sleep undisturbed.
Things will look better in the mornin'.

Antiphony of Judgment for Two Voices
For Linda Brown

He wanted to throw her out of the church.
        He did? Lord have mercy.
Said her dress was so thin,
you could read the word o' God through it.
        Heavenly Days!
He didn't like long sermons.
One day he got up in the middle of one –
said we'd been there long enough,
and closed ever window
in the church house,
and it July!!
        Goodness gracious.

People was just a fannin'
with them funeral home fans.
But that preacher just kept on preachin'.
I reckon he thought the heat in the room
would give 'em a dose of the heat to come
 if'n they didn't repent.
        Lord help us all.

She sat there a minute in that flimsy dress,
fannin' herself with a picture of Jesus.
Said she was hotter than a June bride in a feather bed,
and left.
Paraded herself right out of that church house
while the preacher was still a-preachin'.
About hellfire.
        Well, tarnation!

A Patch of Sun

I sit here in the only patch of sunlight
on a deep and shady trail.
The leaves are silent now.
Not long ago they crackled as I walked.
Now, only their companions
who have not suffered the fall from trees
sing to me, played by a music-maker wind.
The light moves quickly across the path.
The trail darkens.

And I think of you,
the ocean woman whose eyes search
for the accessible horizon
and the light moving on the water;
the surfing woman who has in her bones
not the song of wind in trees
but of the surf on the beach
and the humming sound of foam
as it dissipates across the sand;
the blond woman whose hair is the
color of sand lightened by sun and wind.
You are the heliotrope
who wants no time in the shadowed valley,
in the steep ravines.
You would seek the single patch of sun
in the whispering mountain gloom.

The Stranger

I know about fear of the Stranger.
I **am** the Stranger,
      stranger than fiction
      stranger than the truth
      you think you know,
      in the bright light of neat ruffled houses,
      where one ought
      to be in bed
      and
      one ought
      not be down the street.

I'm the ought not,
      the one who does what
      you would not,
      but wish you could do.

I'm the one you fear,
      the one
      stalked by night
      by bigots and begetters;
      the one who lies awake through your slumber
      and dreams of better days.

I have dual citizenship.

Like Janus I see both directions at once
      in an upside-down delivery system,
      the bizarre sane,
      straightway dangerous . . .
      handled with a chain.

Move on to the River

We could hear the water
as we crouched low among the trees
in the cold damp woods of the night.

Quiet as foxes we were.
Listening.
No dogs barked.

We could hear the river.
No moon.
The stars guided us in the blessed dark.
We had followed the drinking gourd
stumbling north.

"It's not far now," someone said.
A raspy whisper.
No louder than a rustling feather.

Move on to the river.
Move on to the river.
Move on to the river.
And cross the bridge to freedom.

Spirit

Order for the Visitation to the Sick
(In Memory of Robert Francis Kennedy, 1968)

O Lord, reveal, reveal,
        be real.
Steal in a settle down
        and stay a while
        we were yet sinners, God,
        love the world
        so we can love each other.

Mother us out of here
        out of fear
        and carry our sorrows.

Jesus, Savior,
        save your
                our
                children,
                for such is the Kingdom of Heaven.

Grant unto us the joy of thy salvation
        to a nation
        whose relation
        with Thee has died,
        grown cold, old
        things are passed away.

Make them anew.

Song of the Agnostic

God – a word
 as
Sod – a word.
God and sod.

And what of the royal rod
and holy bird?
Did they unite the god and sod?

I never really heard.

Letter to St. Paul

Even with your Gamaliel education
and your speaking with the tongues of Angels,
you struggled with the wholeness of women.

"Wives, submit yourselves unto your husbands . . . .
 Let the women remain silent in the churches," you said.
        We did.

Men built the spires,
        bold Ebenezers to their phallic resurrections
        while silent wombful women reared the sons of God.

("My soul doth magnify the Lord.")

The Breath of God

When the wind blew
out of the breath of God
I moved under the trees
to a more fragrant place.

The breath of Jehovah was rank.
The breath of the Goddess
      like Flowers.

Two Witches

Two
smiling witches
float under the moon,
flying, flying on the broom
of celebration.

October One

Each day the sun moves lower in the sky
 beyond the other side of equinox,
the darker side.
These days we'll have more dark than light.
The air will stiffen
with an autumn cold.
We'll draw our arms around ourselves
to find within our frame
a warmth that's all our own.

The sun is captured in Horizon's greedy need,
kept from our sight
by attitude and circumstance,
by laws we did not legislate
and do not have the power to amend.

Our course is with the sun.
It hides beneath the rim of orange remembering
and keeps us looking now upon the West
and soon upon the East where risen ones bring with them
sometimes less than what we'd hoped, a light that's all our own.

From All Saints to Advent
("Christ in you the hope of Glory." Colossians 1:27)

The world moves closer to the rim
of shadows and of shade.
In moonlight
black branches crack against the sky,
an aging china cup that will not break,
though creased with too much use
and too much expectation.

By day
the skies will turn that clearest, briefest blue,
the color of the virgin
that makes us lift our chins toward heaven,
though we, unlike the legend, have known far more
of Eros and of passion's aching need than she.

We will move with the sun
to darker, darker days
toward Christmas tide
when in the dim and silent caverns
of the heart we search for someone
coming to us,
out of where we thought should be the source
of settled issues, answered questions,
a savior who will lighten up with fullness
the spaces that we cannot fill alone.

Yet now we each must be a Mary to ourselves;
and, not relying on the virgin's womb,
we must conceive the Christ within
so from that space can then emerge a savior
who is not only Christ, the Lord,
but our own fresh unfolding,
the spirit of who we are,
the savior sprung from our own wombs.
And, so, we save ourselves.

My Layers Fall Away

My layers fall away
like onions
tearfully
falling away to the center, to the core
where nothing and all become One.

Suellen Alfred is a retired Professor Emerita from Tennessee Technological University. She lives in Cookeville, Tennessee.

www.ingramcontent.com/pod-product-compliance
Lightning Source LLC
Chambersburg PA
CBHW072104290426
44110CB00014B/1824